Flashes

Hannah Goodfellow

BookLeaf Publishing

Presentation by *BookLeaf Publishing*

Web: www.bookleafpub.com

E-mail: info@bookleafpub.com

ISBN: 9789357212588

First edition 2023

They Hold Me

I sit with my sisters,
entwined are our souls,
understood are the words spoken.

Past life roaming
we explore the places
where we had met before.

We know the pain, the passion and the portrayals
that have defined us,
broken us down and built us back up.

It is the safety
in these moments,
that means the most.

With the warmth of love
cloaking us,
we soften into each other.

One by one, we stand.
I stand…
And the candle flickers,
the light shakes.

"I see you",
an echo of warmth and celebration
ripples through our circle.
And I crack open.

They hold me.
I resist.
They hold me just the same.

The space is still and sacred,
and the world ceases outside.
Flashes of it all in my mind,
emotion roaring in my throat.

"Let me out!"

I feel, I cry, I desire, I dream…
it is all welcome here.

All of me is welcome here.

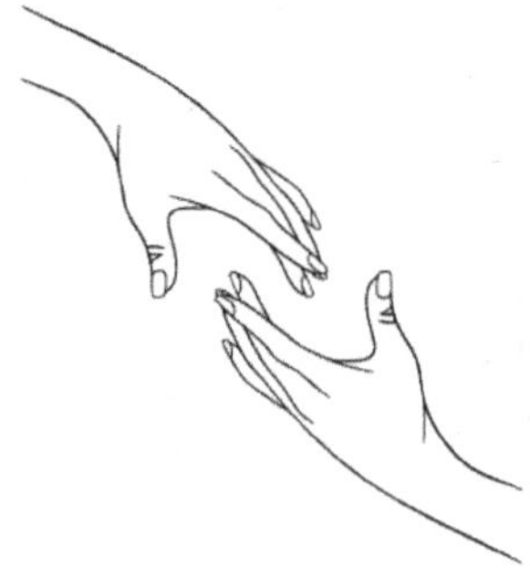

Unheeded Words

Wisdom found me that day
and it filled the void of
uncertainty and frustration
with compassion.
"The mess is the lesson".

Her voice softened into my skin
and filled up the cracks.
A warmth I'd been missing found me
and I sunk in further,
finally listening to the familiar
but unheeded words.

Patience is a project
we are all assigned,
at fated moments
and stretching eras.

Grounded in my body
and I feel the ever-present passion burn.
We sit together in the garden of my mind,
a little overgrown but oh so beautiful.
It's not about the lookout
only the sunflowers, weeds
and the rustle underfoot of the path.

I have hope
and I surrender to the void.
It's an expansive, wings activated
type of heartbeat with me now.
I will fall, I will fly
and I will grab life with both hands.

I will always try.
I will always lean in.

Polaroid

The messages
and that crinkle in your smile.
I reached for your hand
and now you reach for mine.

Wine-stained lips,
trips
and a flash within
that made me believe…

This will be the polaroid of the beginning.

Pause

Found in this moment of pain,
we witness the human condition.
Sadness crashes into us
only we can't swerve
from the fragility of our presence here.

If I lay and listen,
I can hear the hopelessness.
I can feel the heaviness of a heart
united with another.

To be in this loss is excruciating,
it pauses all plans.
But then, as if unaware
time resumes and the world continues.

Moments in our world
are now filled with shakily spoken words,
and we hold on to importance and each other.

Memories are spread across the pages,
glossy photographs
and captures of our heart's laughter.

This is my importance.

The people who receive the call
in celebration, comfort, and chaos of life,
they are my importance.

I find them and they find me.
We hold each other and love each other through
it.

Pause. I understand.
I pause to prioritise life with them.

Armour

Flashes of spiky and sharp words,
created wounds in my heart space.
Hurt and unhealed, I hurled them back.

We were the perpetrators of pain
lodging deep down,
the stories we didn't want to believe,
and trying to escape
the race we never wanted to run.

Swords drawn
and words poised for attack.
If we saw beauty,
we'd swing.

I wish we'd known back then.
I wish we'd known we could drop the swords
and help each other rise.

And now we know,
the battle is over
and our growth is safe, seen & celebrated.

A flash of the words that wounded
rise in me sometimes.

I know there's no battle,
so, I lift my sword and cut the tie
that held me in the fight.

It all falls away,
and I find them.

They look different with their armour off.
Beautiful.

Speakerphone

The night is numb, quiet…
yet filled with the artificial echo of
speakerphone.

What is coming next?
I know what's coming next.
We've both known.

An icy flash of fear has spread through my body
and left my heart cold.
I can see the night sky on my bed,
I trace the shapes and hold my breath.

I hear the words
that sting confirmation into the years of
"unlovable".
They cut me, crack me open
and then come back to do it all again.

The moment goes on and on and on…
and you wait,
for the rivers to flow and fill up my room.

Instead, I question everything
and remind myself to breathe.

With each 'why', we feel further apart.
With each minute, you fade further away.
With each breath, I am back on my bed…
tracing the night sky.

I am cut deeper by the shrill echo of the speaker.

For a moment,
it's a painful silence,
then the night goes on,
and it's just the pain.

Clarity

The tightness finds my chest,
I feel it all close in.
Nothing makes it better
but when I venture to the water,
it's clear.

Vulnerability

She wraps herself in the warmth of trust,
grounds herself
and breathes into the words that are rising.

They rise in her throat
and overflow into the moment,
holding their own and taking up space.

Her heart cracks open
and as she stands in the light of vulnerability,
she notices a highway of freedom
unfolding before her.
Her journey along the road,
is illuminated by flashes of light.

An atmosphere of honesty in her heart,
she knows the mask must go.
Peering at her reflection
her hands rise naturally
and draw away the veil.

She can feel the air on her skin
and the rarity of being seen.
Fear and yet freedom.

She steps forward
claiming it as hers,
claiming it as truth,
claiming it as safe.

Earth Angels

She longed to be known,
not by bright lights
or an increasing number on a screen,
but by the earth angels, just like her,
who understood the depth of her soul.

She declared the shadow and the light her friend,
making space for holding herself
with love, kindness and respect.

Often, she'd find herself with fiery flashes of
words
and the warmth of a white light supporting her.
Grateful for those midnight moments,
she would amplify their power and permanence
and mark them in pen.

Her feelings that had once lay dormant,
were waking up.
Her beauty that was hidden,
was stepping forward into the light.
And her voice once muffled by fear,
was rising to be heard.

She called forward her sisters
and they walked the road back home.

Sister Soul

We ruminate in our space,
magnetising our desires
and dreaming of the days we've worked for.

We build our vision each day,
pausing for reflections, celebration
and hysterical synchronicities.

Utterly seen is your soul, as is mine.
You are my reflector, storyteller
and break from the world,
as we hold the space in laughter and love.

Conversations from our inner world
are woven into my memory for evermore.
Lyrics, love of all kinds
and life that has spun us in all directions.
The stretches of time never measured
and the nights you held my hand
are here in my heart.

Our space is the same
and yet different now,
as we journey toward new beginnings
and the moments we always knew we'd reach.

I imagine what's ahead is a flash of change
and we'll never expect the blessings that will
find us.
But for now, I'm pausing,
to remember the times, we spoke to the sky
and whispered into the night.

Sister soul, everything we desire is ours.
I know, because I once prayed for you.

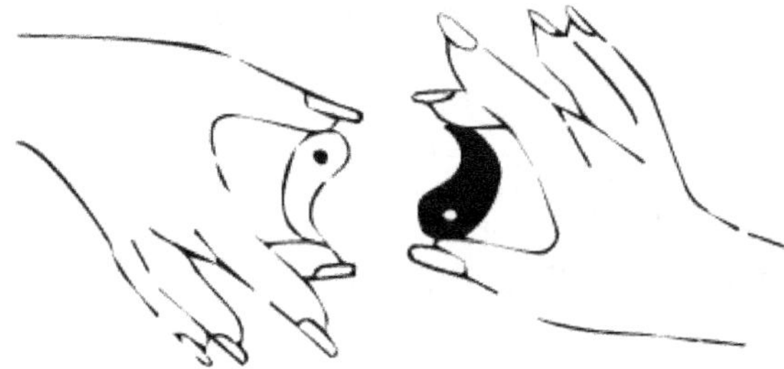

My Sweet Flower

In the still afternoon,
I talk to myself and say…

Allow the breeze to carry you,
My sweet flower.
It will take you to
divine and daring places
you never knew you needed to go.

Ride the breeze,
to find joy and adventure,
they'll allow you to know yourself deeply.

A serene sunset on my skin,
my eyes remain closed
and my mind whispers…

I am the flower.
Cracked open and blossoming.
Always unfolding.
Delicate, vibrant, and trusting.

I am the flower.

Ripples of Resonance

A touch to my lips allows them to part,
curiosity runs over the portal to my voice.
What is there had been forgotten,
hidden,
dimmed,
quietened,
But now, it feels different,
I choose different.

I welcome the words,
activating them softly…
Slowly.

Whispering,
they venture out into the open.
The words swell over a passer-by
and their skin is covered
with ripples of resonance.

Sacred Simplicity

A welcome breeze,
crunching leaves
and the safety of the sunset
replays as I visit here each day.

My chest rises and falls,
like the rhythm of the ocean.
The adventure and stretches of life will expand
me.
Perpetually and lovingly,
they invite me to lean in.

I put words to the page,
they come and they go
with shining rays and shadowy lows.

Today, I rise with confidence.
Tomorrow, I lean into the release of fear.
Another sun tickles the horizon
and I drop my pen for now.

Wading into the water
I feel the mess of it all fade away.
I float on the surface,
soothed by the sky
and cleansed by the sea.

I emerge at the same place,
the place made for me.
Each moment, made for me...
to decide.

"where do I desire to arrive?"
"what do I crave to feel along the way?"

Flash. I get to decide.

You get to decide.

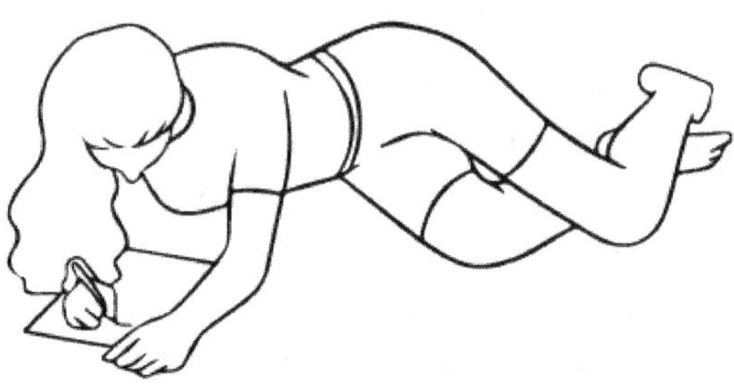

22

Radical Protest

The division and hate,
it's easy to be bothered,
to be angry.
Anger is not my long-term solution,
but needed for now.
After a while it turns the war outside inside
and wreaks further havoc.

Healing and held space are the
compassionate and radical protest.
My eyes and ears remain open
to injustice and pain.
My heart and mind remain curious
to learning and growth.

My focus is returning to my power.
Moments of breath fill my bank,
inching closer to my truth.

When I expand my ability to love deeply
I am wiser.
And so, we all are.

Let's explore together and come back home.

Cherished

Memories of home
in rolling hills,
when dusk would fall
and I'd talk to the sky
in a plaid skirt.

This is what I did,
and what I want,
but mostly
I am lonely
and I'm not sure I belong.

I'd sit in the solitude,
fall apart in tears,
two ears would lick my fingers
and beg me to follow.

There was an escape in the breeze
and bug chasing,
I'd soak up the daylight,
running till my chest hurt
and my legs ached.

A plee for clean hands
and a return to indoors

would draw me unwillingly.
But with the warmth of clean water
and love on the table,
I was no longer lost,
I was cherished and savoured.

Sit With Me

You sit with me,
and listen to the waves.

You lie under the sun with me,
as our feet embrace the grass
and my heart cracks open to yours.

Delicious is this breeze caressing my skin,
and the way our laughter floats
toward the clouds.
The rays surround the sun
and flash a brilliant calm into this moment.

Saltwater flows between our toes
and the world passes by around us,
with its own intricate beauty
and soulful stories.

You bring me here,
to my peaceful place,
when I need it most,
just because
and to celebrate being together.

With you, here,
I feel safe, home and open,
watching clouds and exploring the sky…
and our future.

Curious of Fear

Don't judge or push away
the fear in a pursuit of lightness.
Fear finds us with reason
and while it may not drive the road home
its presence is a teacher.

I will continue to embolden myself
in fearful moments
to reach for curiosity
and expand into the space
in which fear can be heard, felt, and seen.

Magnetic

I am safe in this moment
and each one that follows.
My soul is magnetic and infinite,
a galaxy of stars thrives within me.

Past, present and future me,
I hold you in my arms
and pray that you always feel my unconditional
love.

I welcome deep and powerful breath
into my body.

More breath allows me to soften,
to open.
I remember the truth within me.
Opportunity. Ease. Compassion.

It is all within me.
It is always finding me.
I am powerfully supported by the Divine.

Soaring in Surrender

I was made to succeed, shine, and soar.

The void,
the mystery and the surrender to the process,
is where I feel and heal.

It is where I come to open my heart.

As I lean in,
I discover my power waiting beneath the
surface,
for me to crack myself open and be seen.

I see the goddess
who magnetises her every desire.

In this space,
I discover all of it,
everything I ever wanted,
accessible to my heart and hands.

I affirm to my heart,
it is possible for me
to shine and soar and succeed.
It is part of my soul's purpose here on Earth.

Flashes of success hit my heart,
and I rise with the knowing,
I have shone and soared the whole time.

Reflections

I am perfect.
Every cell, scar, inch of my skin
made sacred
and my kindness etched
within the memories of my loves.

I may not always see it...
the beauty and the divine power,
the depth of knowing and peaceful grace.
I may not always see it,
But the quiet passion for my reflection is there.

Within my heart's walls
is my wildness,
rising to be unleashed
and to remind us all, of the truth.

In times of transparency,
I listen to my desire
to witness the world
that I deeply understand
and don't, all at once.

Dancing toward the gateway
of growth,

I move with my knowing
and rise on my toes.
They ache after each expansion,
and still, I revel in the delicate perfection
that is this life of growth.

I am perfect.
The discomfort is divine,
and the resistance, a temporary fixture.
I cherish the space in which I reflect
and honour the flashes of lightness
with illuminating tenderness.

I am perfect.
I am rising.
I am seen.

Unconditional Midnight

I've found home in myself so many times.
Over and over again,
I've come back home to this place.

It's a sudden moment of peace
yet joy and pleasure
that floods my body
in an unmistakable likelihood of transformation.

It is an unmistakable knowing,
that what is filling my body is not just good
but the merging and making of something
much more beautiful than good.
It holds the good and the bad together,
giving grace, acceptance and love to the lessons,
the pain and the pieces
that once felt unbearable and dark.

The darkness meets its light and lessons
And they don't dissipate or reduce each other,
instead, they tuck around each other's corners
and fill the cracks made perfectly to be filled.

They don't try to change
or lessen
or use their own attributes to "help".
They wrap around the space
with love
and they stay there,
unconditionally.